First published 1984
The Post Office
22/25 Finsbury Square London EC2A 1PH

© The Post Office London

All rights reserved

No part of this publication may be reproduced,
stored in a retrieval system or transmitted
in any form or by any means electronic,
mechanical, photocopying, recording or otherwise,
without the prior permission of the
publishers.

Designed by Carroll & Dempsey Limited

Special photography by Phil Sayer

Text by Mike Barden, Woods Barden Associates Limited

Printed in the United Kingdom by
Jolly & Barber Limited, Rugby, Warwickshire

ISBN 0 946165 01 7

CONTENTS

HERALDRY · 4
CATTLE · 6
URBAN RENEWAL · 8
EUROPA · 10
ECONOMIC SUMMIT · 12
GREENWICH MERIDIAN · 14
ROYAL MAIL · 17
BRITISH COUNCIL · 20
CHRISTMAS · 22
ACKNOWLEDGEMENTS · 24
STAMP POSITIONING GUIDE · 24

INTRODUCTION

Each year's stamp programme provides the opportunity to reflect our national heritage, achievements and contributions to the world at large. The stamps in this book will be remembered, not only for their varied and topical themes, but also for the way in which they mirror the immense diversity of design talents available in Britain today.

All the Royal Mail Special Stamps produced during 1984, and the interesting stories behind their themes, designs, and production, are brought together in this special book which will serve as a cherished record of a year in British postage stamp history.

ROYAL MAIL SPECIAL STAMPS · 1984

HERALDRY

In today's technological age, Jeffery Matthews stands out as a man imbued with a very keen sense of history and tradition. His enthusiasm for our heritage, however, is far from being a simple nostalgia for days gone by; in fact, it has much more to do with the relevance Jeffery believes yesterday's values have today, even with all our modern technology. And nowhere has he given clearer or better expression of his credo than in the design of the Heraldry stamps.

To many people heraldry conjures up a romantic image of knights of old; jousts and tournaments; chivalry and pageantry. To Jeffery it is all of these things, and much more besides. For he sees heraldry as one of the most comprehensive systems of sign language ever invented, a symbolic medium to which present-day graphic design owes a great debt. It lives on in its own right through the College of Arms whose 500th anniversary these stamps commemorate.

From his earliest days at art college, Jeffery has been fascinated by heraldry and lettering – a fascination reflected in much of his work over the years.

THE FAMOUS FENWICK ROLL
COMPILED ABOUT 1550
CONTAINS OVER 1,000 COATS OF ARMS

This ranges from the designs, with their heraldic symbolism, for the first decimal definitive issues for Scotland, Wales, Northern Ireland and the Isle of Man in 1971, and the value lettering for these and current definitive stamps, to the hand-drawn masthead lettering and coat of arms which are a familiar sight on the front page of *The Sunday Times* newspaper.

Traditions and craftsmanship have been facts of life for Jeffery Matthews since he was a schoolboy. His father Henry, 'Freeman, Citizen and Goldsmith of London', ran a gold watch case making business in Clerkenwell, London; the young Matthews spent a great deal of his spare time helping his father in the workshop, learning the art of the master craftsman in the process.

The Matthews family, in fact, can trace its history back to the sixteenth century when 'Fine Knives' were made in England by Richard Matthews on Fleet Bridge in 1563. The family business of gold watch case making was established by Jeffery's great grandfather in 1818 and has been handed down through successive generations to his brother, Martin, who continues the craft today.

Inheriting such a tradition, Jeffery, not surprisingly, has made his own contribution to the family's reputation for craftsmanship. In recent years, while continuing his graphic design practice, he has become increasingly involved in carving slate pendants and paper-weights as well as wood engraving bookplates, letterheadings, watch-papers and greetings cards which he prints on a hand-operated antique Albion press.

Graphic design, however, remains his first love. What he finds particularly gratifying is the fact that he may well have laid the foundations for a new tradition in the Matthews family since his daughter, son and daughter-in-law are all freelance graphic designers themselves – the whole family often collaborating on design projects.

Family collaboration has played a significant part in Jeffery's success in stamp design. His wife Chris, who writes under the name of Charity Boxall, has worked closely with him on a number of Royal Mail stamps, including the twenty-fifth anniversary of the Coronation in 1978 and the Royal Wedding in 1981. For these issues, Chris wrote the text for the First Day Cover filler cards, presentation packs and souvenir booklets which Jeffery designed.

This husband-and-wife teamwork was again seen to good effect on the Heraldry stamp issue, with Chris assisting in the research and providing the words for Jeffery's presentation pack design.

Jeffery's research into heraldry took him to the College of Arms in the City of London. With the help of the Officers of Arms, today's custodians of the use of heraldry and direct successors to the heralds who marshalled the nobility at Royal tournaments and ceremonies in medieval times, he was able to delve into the college's extensive and unique archives. His research also took him to the Tower of London where the famous Herald's Museum collection is housed.

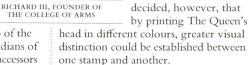

RICHARD III, FOUNDER OF THE COLLEGE OF ARMS

FROM OUTLINE CONCEPT TO FINAL ARTWORK – HOW JEFFERY MATTHEWS DEVELOPED THE ARMS OF THE EARL MARSHAL

From the outset, Jeffery aimed to incorporate historical aspects of the Quincentenary into his designs in the most logical order possible. When he had completed his research, this aim was given practical expression in the subjects he chose for the four stamps. The arms of the College and of its founder in 1484, Richard III, were fairly obvious choices. To these were added the arms of the Earl Marshal, the Duke of Norfolk, because of his special position on royal ceremonial protocol and the arms of the City of London where the College was founded and still functions.

In his original designs, Jeffery had intended to have The Queen's head printed in gold or silver to complement the golds and silvers in the coats of arms used. It was later decided, however, that by printing The Queen's head in different colours, greater visual distinction could be established between one stamp and another.

Although the written description of a coat of arms is exact and given in precise order, the artist has a great deal of freedom in how he interprets this. Taking advantage of this freedom, Jeffery was able to manipulate the designs in such a way that the coat of arms on each stamp occupied a similar area of space.

THE EARL MARSHAL HOLDS A SPECIAL RESPONSIBILITY FOR ROYAL CEREMONIAL OCCASIONS, THE HIGHLIGHT OF THESE BEING ROYAL CORONATIONS

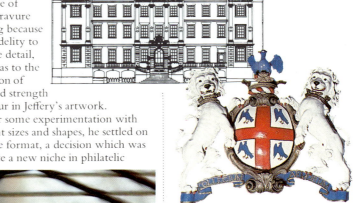

THE COLLEGE OF ARMS AND AN 18TH CENTURY CARVING OF ITS COAT OF ARMS

The shield is the essential feature of a coat of arms; Jeffery, in fact could well have concentrated on this aspect to the exclusion of all other elements. He decided, however, that it was more appropriate to interpret the crests, helms, supporters and mottoes in the way these have evolved over the centuries.

Supporters, for example, appear on three of the stamps – these are the dragons, lions or horses standing either side of the shields. Since supporters were not an established element of Richard III's coat of arms, Jeffery concentrated instead on a highly decorative interpretation of the red and ermine mantling which emanates from under the crown over the helmet. The mantling, incidentally, was a head cloth originally worn by the Crusaders to protect them from the sun.

Jeffery's range of artistic licence on this work is clearly demonstrated by the contrast between the abbreviated coat of arms on the 16p stamp and the very detailed design of the Earl Marshal's coat of arms on the 28p stamp.

The final reproduction is an excellent example of photogravure printing because of its fidelity to this fine detail, as well as to the gradation of tone and strength of colour in Jeffery's artwork.

After some experimentation with different sizes and shapes, he settled on a square format, a decision which was to create a new niche in philatelic history for it resulted in the very first square Royal Mail special stamps ever issued. Philatelic history perhaps has had few more appropriate makers!

JEFFERY MATTHEWS – FASCINATED BY HERALDRY AND LETTERING SINCE HIS ART COLLEGE DAYS

HERALDRY

Date of issue: 17 January 1984

The four stamps were designed by Jeffery Matthews FSIAD and printed in photogravure by Harrison & Sons (High Wycombe) Limited.

Format:	square
Size:	34.7mm × 34.7mm
Perforations:	14½ × 14½
Number per sheet:	100
Paper:	unwatermarked phosphor coated
Gum:	PVA Dextrin

CATTLE

PREVIOUS EXPERIENCE IN STAMPS is sometimes an important factor in the choice of designer or illustrator. What is generally of more importance, however, is the designer or illustrator's experience in the subject chosen for a particular stamp issue. There is probably no better example of the success of this policy than Barry Driscoll's majestic portraits for the British Cattle stamp issue – an issue which commemorates both the centenary of the Highland Cattle Society and the bicentenary of the Royal Highland and Agricultural Society of Scotland.

Although Barry had no previous experience of stamp design whatsoever, there are few living British artists with better credentials for animal life portraiture than him. Born in Dulwich in 1926, he traces his love of wildlife back to his wartime childhood which was spent in the Shropshire countryside. A series of prestigious commissions from London Zoo and the World Wild Life Fund later on secured his place as a foremost illustrator in his field. He was also chosen by Henry Williamson to illustrate a special limited edition of *Tarka the Otter* and has worked on several books with zoologist Desmond Morris.

At his home in Kingsclere, Berkshire, Barry continues to work on a project which has been close to his heart for many years – namely, a definitive work covering all the mammals of Britain and North America. This vast project has been the subject of his brush and palette for seven years and he believes that he is still years from completion.

It was a series of Barry's paintings of British sheep breeds, in fact, that brought him to the attention of The Post Office and led, ultimately, to his commission on this stamp issue. He had spent three years tracking down, photographing and painting elusive and rare breeds of sheep, masterpieces which now grace the walls of his home. His approach to the cattle assignment was the same as for the sheep – meticulous in every detail and demonstrating an unashamed dedication to the subject.

The Highland cow with its ruggedness is featured on the first stamp in the series. Able to forage in sparsely vegetated areas, this breed is famed for its hardiness and adaptability, its long shaggy coat and short thick undercoat providing protection against extremes of cold and heat.

While Highland cattle may be found in a variety of colours ranging from black to silver dun, it is best known as having a reddish tinge as represented in Barry Driscoll's portrait. There it stands with windswept coat and sturdy frame set four-square to the elements and surrounded by the magnificent Scottish Highlands.

The Highland Cattle Society was founded in 1884 and its dedication to the breed has resulted in Highland cattle being exported throughout the Northern hemisphere as well as to Australasia. The strong mothering instincts of the cow, coupled with excellent beef yields and low management overheads, have contributed to the success of Highland cattle as cross breeds with other strains.

When Barry Driscoll visited Chillingham Park to make his preliminary sketches of the legendary wild white bull for the second stamp, he soon discovered that the adjective 'wild' meant exactly that. For the sleek dainty appearance of this unique breed belies an untamed, aggressive temperament; bulls will attack any human who ventures too close. Consequently, Barry had to remain at a respectful distance from his quarry, in the vigilant company of a warden trained to recognise any danger signals.

The Chillingham cattle are believed to derive directly from the wild Auroch (a type of ox) which roamed around these islands prior to the introduction of domestic breeds by the Romans. It is over 700 years since a wild herd of these white cattle from the Medieval Caledonian forest was corralled behind the stone walls of the Chillingham estate for the hunt. Today, Chillingham Park is administered by the Chillingham Wild Cattle Association and is the only place where this unique herd may be seen.

Inbreeding over 700 years does not seem to have weakened the Chillingham strain, a fact probably due to the leadership of the herd by a 'king' bull who is the strongest and fittest in the group. The king bull's reign is absolute, even to the siring of all calves, although this right is often challenged by jealous rivals. The outcome is usually a spectacular yet bloodless fight where male pride, or loss of it, is the determining factor.

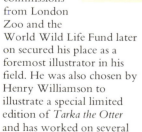

THE ARTIST BARRY DRISCOLL

TWO CONTRASTING EXAMPLES OF THE ARTIST'S WORK 'TARKA THE OTTER' TITLE PAGE (ABOVE LEFT) AND ROUGH FELL RAM IN ITS TYPICALLY HARSH HABITAT

DETAIL FROM DRISCOLL'S ORIGINAL PAINTING OF THE HIGHLAND COW SHOWN ACTUAL SIZE

In the finished stamp Barry has managed to capture not only the menacing wariness of the bulls but has also recorded in the background some of the ancient oaks for which Chillingham Park is renowned.

ROYAL MAIL SPECIAL STAMPS · 1984

For the third stamp in the series Barry paid a visit to Newbury Cattle Show to sketch a classic example of a Hereford bull. This muscularly handsome yet docile beast is the product of 200 years of intensive breeding in which technology has lent a helping hand to yield a prolific breeder that combines hardiness with early maturity and the ability to convert grass rapidly into prime beef.

The Hereford Herd Book Society was founded in 1878 and today presides over a breeding programme still centred in Hereford that can boast the world's most widely distributed beef stock. Over five million cattle are now registered in fifty-six countries throughout the world and breeders are internationally linked together through the World Hereford Council formed in 1955.

While on location in Snowdonia looking for the Welsh Black bull, Barry was lucky enough to spot a striking example of the breed as it stood appropriately posed against its natural habitat of rugged Welsh mountains – a lucky scoop that saved him hours of patient searching.

The Welsh Black has been the native breed of Wales since pre-Roman times. Today, thanks to the efforts of the Welsh Black Cattle Society, formed in 1873, the breed combines the features found in the small North Wales animal with the larger South Wales or Castlemartin strain.

The resultant breed has a deep long low set body with a strong bone structure and thick coat varying in colour from rusty to jet black. The cows have a strong mothering instinct due to the need to protect their young from the hostile environment experienced by this hardy hill breed.

DRISCOLL REFERENCE PHOTOGRAPH TAKEN AT NEWBURY CATTLE SHOW

These cattle can survive harsh winters with little cover and sparse rations. Black bulls are found today throughout the world, coping with climates as disparate as those of Saudi Arabia and Canada and prospering without the need for expensive feed.

The last stamp in the series depicts the Irish Moiled cow which is claimed to be the oldest surviving breed in the United Kingdom. The word 'moiled' is an anglicised version of the old gaelic word 'mael' meaning bald, indicating its lack of horns. Barry has placed his example of the Irish Moiled Cow in front of the Legananny Dolmen, a megalithic tomb dating from about 3000 BC situated near Ballynahinch, County Down.

As recently as two years ago, this Irish breed was virtually extinct with less than a dozen pure bred cattle remaining. Now thanks to the strenuous efforts of Belfast Zoo, where Barry executed his preliminary sketches, the National Trust, the Rare Breed Survival Trust and a handful of dedicated breeders, the Irish 'Moilie' seems to be out of danger. It is hoped that by 1986 its name will no longer be on the list of 'most endangered species'.

Barry liaised closely with the relevant breeds associations while working on this set of stamps to ensure that he correctly represented each bloodline. It is absolutely essential to do this as each breed society, whether of cattle, dogs or cats, usually has strict rules about how an animal should be portrayed.

While most stamp artwork is executed at four times stamp size, Barry preferred to work on a much larger canvas. Despite this, the final reproduction has retained all the fine detail and texture of his paintings of these magnificent animals – a testimony to both Barry's skills and Harrison's photogravure process.

ANIMAL PORTRAITURE OF AN EARLIER ERA
'FARMER WITH HIS PRIZE HEIFER'
BY AN UNKNOWN ARTIST (CIRCA 1830)

CATTLE	
Date of issue: 6 March 1984 The five stamps were designed by Barry Driscoll ARCA and printed in photogravure by Harrison & Sons (High Wycombe) Limited.	
Format: horizontal	
Size: 41mm x 30mm	
Perforations: 15 x 14	
Number per sheet: 100	
Paper: unwatermarked phosphor coated	
Gum: PVA Dextrin	

URBAN RENEWAL

Urban renewal was a very appropriate stamp theme in 1984 because the year heralded the opening of one of the most imaginative urban renewal projects yet seen in Britain – the International Garden Festival site in Liverpool. The year also celebrated the 150th anniversaries of the Royal Institute of British Architects and the Chartered Institute of Building which play a vital role in the renewal of our urban landscapes.

The extent and style of urban growth and renewal in any period of our history has invariably been closely related to the level of economic activity as well as to public attitudes prevailing at the time.

Today, following much unbridled property development and misguided town planning in the postwar period, there is a much keener public scepticism of our planners' infallibility. This, combined with the effects of economic recession, has forced planners to look more at the concept of urban renewal and less at urban redevelopment; in essence, the aim now is to find ways of retaining the unique characters of our cities while improving their environments as efficient and usable places for work and leisure.

Each of the subjects chosen to highlight aspects of urban renewal in these stamps exemplifies this new, more sympathetic attitude to the real needs and aspirations of people who live and work in urban environments.

The Liverpool International Garden Festival project featured on the 16p stamp is a powerful demonstration of what can be done to regenerate even the most derelict urban areas. For what was nothing less than a stagnant wasteland has been completely transformed into a showpiece public amenity.

THE TRICKETT & WEBB DESIGN TEAM WERE ABLE TO CALL UPON THEIR EXPERIENCE IN HIGH-QUALITY ARCHITECTURAL GRAPHICS

TRICKETT & WEBB'S ORIGINAL CONCEPT OF SHOWING PARTIALLY UNROLLED ARCHITECTURAL PLANS LAID OVER PHOTOGRAPHS

Following the six-month garden festival, half the site will become a permanent public park, the splendid Festival Building designed by Arup Associates will be converted into a sports and leisure centre and the rest will provide an attractive landscaped area for housing, industrial and commercial developments.

The 20½p stamp features the Milburngate Shopping Centre in Durham, an excellent example of how, with sensitive design and careful choice of materials, new developments can be made to blend with buildings of a bygone era. Designed by Building Design Partnership, the new centre has been constructed with materials such as dark coloured bricks and natural slate roofs in a way that respects the scale and historic significance of its surroundings. The end result is a very functional and pleasing harmonisation of old and new.

An entirely different aspect of urban renewal is highlighted in the 28p stamp. With the decline of some traditional industries, many parts of the country face the problem of how to regenerate inner city industrial sites which have outlived their original purpose. The Bristol City Docks scheme is a typical example of the problem – and a lesson in how to achieve an imaginative solution.

A casualty of changing methods in marine transportation, these docks in the heart of the city fell into disuse to leave an unwelcome and unsightly legacy of decaying warehouses and storage sheds. The City Council's answer was to refurbish these facilities for an entirely new purpose. Now ten years later, the area is once again a bustling focus for the city with a radio station, exhibition hall, museum, art gallery, shops, riverside walkways, sailing centre and river ferry service.

The building shown – Bush House – was refurbished by JT Design Build, and was designed to house both their offices and the Arnolfini Gallery.

THE MADDOX CONCEPT TAKES SHAPE, FROM PENCIL SKETCH TO PEN AND FINALLY TO COLOUR

The housing development in Perth featured on the 31p stamp demonstrates how new urban environments can be created in total harmony with existing town architecture. Designed by James Parr and Partners, the new buildings are of various heights to re-create the complexity of older developments, houses are set back from one another and roofs run at different angles to create a visual change of pace.

Urban renewal is a subject very close to Ronald Maddox's heart for over the last twenty years his paintings and drawings have reflected his love for the form and colour of the British landscape and the architecture which is complementary to that landscape. His previous experience was particularly relevant since he designed the Village Churches stamps in 1972 and the British Historic Buildings issue in 1978.

A VALUABLE REFERENCE FOR RONALD MADDOX WAS THIS THREE-DIMENSIONAL COMPUTER MODEL OF THE LIVERPOOL GARDEN FESTIVAL BUILDING

Following consultation with the Civic Trust and RIBA, and with the architects of various schemes, most of his original research was carried out on location, involving both pencil drawings and colour sketches. Alternative locations such as Covent Garden, London, Norwich and Newcastle were included but the final selection was eventually reduced to the four locations shown on the stamps.

Meanwhile, the Trickett & Webb Design Group was pursuing an entirely different approach. The company, headed by

TRICKETT & WEBB AND RONALD MADDOX ALSO JOINED FORCES ON THE FIRST DAY COVER AND PRESENTATION PACK

Lynn Trickett and Brian Webb, is one of London's most successful graphic design groups with several Designer and Art Directors Association (D&AD) awards to its credit. Through its association with Trickett Associates, architects, the group had established a reputation for high quality architectural graphics and exhibition projects.

Trickett & Webb also researched the project independently through the Civic Trust and a number of architectural firms, their aim being to combine aspects of urban renewal with its relevant architectural dimension. From this, the idea was developed to show partially unrolled architectural plans laid over illustrations and photographs of completed projects.

Both designs were favourably received by the Stamp Advisory Committee and the outcome was that Ronald Maddox and Trickett & Webb were asked to combine their design ideas. A factor in this decision was that the Liverpool International Garden Festival project was still under construction, thereby ruling out the idea of photographs. This collaborative effort was carried right through to the first day covers and presentation pack which were designed by Trickett & Webb and illustrated by Ronald Maddox.

Each of the participants had to modify their original designs to accommodate the other's concepts. One of the first tasks, for example, was to ensure that the aspect shown in the architectural plans matched the angle of view in each of the illustrations.

The introduction of the overlay, of course, meant that essential parts of Ronald Maddox's original illustrations would have been obscured. Consequently, he decided to re-illustrate the four subjects to ensure they would be centred within the illustrative area. Although this meant smaller illustrations, he managed to retain almost all of the meticulous detail of his original paintings.

The biggest problem of all was posed by the Liverpool Garden Festival Building illustration which had to be developed in line with construction progress on the project.

Ronald visited the site whilst construction and landscaping were in progress. With the co-operation of the Royal Academy, where Arup Associates' model of the building was on display, he was able to make drawings for the stamp artwork and produce a detailed illustration which is faithful to the completed building.

ILLUSTRATOR RONALD MADDOX – REFLECTING A LOVE FOR THE BRITISH LANDSCAPE AND ITS ARCHITECTURE

RESPECT FOR THE SCALE AND CHARACTER OF ITS HISTORICAL SURROUNDINGS (INSET) WAS A VITAL DESIGN CONSIDERATION FOR THE MILBURNGATE SHOPPING CENTRE IN DURHAM

URBAN RENEWAL

Date of issue: 10 April 1984

The four stamps were designed and illustrated by Trickett and Webb Ltd and Ronald Maddox VPRI FSIAD FSAI and printed in photogravure by Harrison & Sons (High Wycombe) Limited.

Format:	horizontal
Size:	41mm x 30mm
Perforations:	15 x 14
Number per sheet:	100
Paper:	unwatermarked phosphor coated
Gum:	PVA Dextrin

EUROPA

While the concept of European unity is not as yet completely fulfilled, the process of closer co-operation among European nations grows stronger. In 1984, two separate events epitomised the closer ties being forged in Europe today and these are marked by this unusual and interesting pair of se-tenant stamps; the Conference of European Postal and Telecommunications Administrations (CEPT) celebrated its twenty-fifth anniversary while, in June, the second election to the European Parliament was held.

These two organisations not only share the common goals of European co-operation but also a common heritage since the CEPT grew out of the postal union established by the member countries of the European Coal and Steel Community (ECSC) whose parliament eventually became the European Parliament.

The CEPT has already had a marked influence on the stamp programmes of all the twenty-six participating European nations, including Britain. Each year, a CEPT theme is established and all member countries interpret this in one issue of their stamp programme for that year. The Folklore stamps of 1981, the British Theatre stamps of 1982 and British Engineering Achievements stamps of 1983 are recent examples of how the Post Office has interpreted the CEPT theme.

This year, because of the CEPT's twenty-fifth anniversary, it was agreed to have a uniform symbolic design in the CEPT stamps issued by all member-countries – this, in fact, had been the policy until 1974. Consequently, an international

THE PALAIS DE L'EUROPE IN STRASBURG, HOME OF THE EUROPEAN PARLIAMENT

competition was held in which thirty-seven designs were submitted by artists from twenty countries. The winning design by Jacky Larrivière representing Monaco uses a simple bridge symbolic of the postal and telecommunications links of the CEPT and includes the CEPT logo of four linked post-horns incorporating the letters CEPT.

The CEPT was formed in 1959 at Montreux in Switzerland and is one of eight regional groupings of the Universal Postal Union (UPU): One of the world's oldest and largest international organisations, the UPU seeks to improve and modernise postal services worldwide without impinging on the internal postal freedom of member nations.

Since the efficiency of modern postal services depends on the closest possible international co-operation, the CEPT has a vital role to play in helping European postal organisations meet the complex needs of what is the most concentrated grouping of developed nations in the world today. Common problems and strategies are resolved at CEPT Plenary Assemblies and through regular meetings of working parties and study groups.

The same ideal of European co-operation is the guiding philosophy of the European Parliament. Originally formed as the European

FRITZ WEGNER WITH JACKY LARRIVIERE, WINNER OF THE CEPT ANNIVERSARY STAMP DESIGN COMPETITION

Coal and Steel Community Parliament in 1952, this became the European Parliament following the Treaties of Rome five years later which created the European Economic Community (EEC) and the European Atomic Energy Commission.

Consisting of 142 members nominated by the national parliaments of the six original EEC member states, the European Parliament increased its representation to 198 when Denmark, Ireland and the United Kingdom joined in 1973.

Six years later, a significant step was taken when voters in all nine countries were given the opportunity to elect 410 members directly to the Parliament. With the accession of Greece to the Community in 1981, representation increased to 434. In 1984

FRITZ WEGNER'S ORIGINAL SQUARE DESIGNS FOR THE EUROPA STAMP

voters in the ten countries had their second opportunity to elect members who will represent the interests of some 270 million people.

In the European Parliament, members usually sit,

FRITZ WEGNER – HIS NINTH ROYAL MAIL COMMISSION

ROYAL MAIL SPECIAL STAMPS · 1984

THIS 1731 'DICTIONARY OF HEATHEN GODS' WAS A USEFUL REFERENCE SOURCE FOR FRITZ WEGNER

not in national blocks, but in one of the seven multinational political groupings where they are able to meet and discuss issues with like-minded representatives from other Community countries. Unlike Westminster, the Parliament does not have the last say on legislation. Its influence on the law-making process, however, is growing and its powers include both the right to dismiss the EEC Commission as a whole and shared authority with the Council of Ministers for the Community Budget. All aspects of Community activity are discussed in debates and committees, with particular attention being paid to co-operation in foreign policy between member countries.

The European Election stamps were designed by Fritz Wegner who also adapted the CEPT stamp from the Larrivière design. Fritz has already been associated with a CEPT stamp before as he designed the Folklore issue in 1981 which was the chosen CEPT theme for that year. This was his ninth Royal Mail commission, his other designs including Christmas 1969 and 1979, Anniversaries in 1970 and 1971, Great Britons in 1974 and Cycling in 1978.

The Europa theme of the CEPT stamps has been complemented by Fritz's interpretation of the story of the Europa mythology in the European Election stamps. His design resulted from the considerable research he undertook into the subject, his richest sources proving to be a 1731 dictionary of *Heathen Gods* and the *Larousse World Mythology* edited by Pierre Grimal.

According to mythology, Europa was the daughter of Agenor, King of Tyre. One day, Zeus saw her playing on the seashore with companions and fell in love with her at once. Disguising himself as a white bull – a feat which managed to frighten off everyone except Europa – he lay down at her feet. Then tempting Europa to climb onto his back, he suddenly arose and swam out to sea, carrying her off to the island of Crete where he resumed his human form. Europa subsequently bore him three sons, one of whom was Minos. The Cretan culture known as Minoan, is often considered as the beginning of European culture as we know it today. The gods later gave Europa in marriage to the King of Crete, Asterius, who adopted the children. After the death of Asterius, Europa was transformed into a constellation.

THE EUROPEAN PARLIAMENT'S 'ESPRIT' PROGRAMME AIMS AT ENSURING THAT EUROPE IS NOT DEPENDENT ON JAPAN AND THE USA FOR TECHNOLOGICAL ADVANCES

Despite checking various references in the British Museum, Fritz found there was no definitive visual representation of the Europa legend. This, of course, meant that he was able to exercise considerable freedom in his interpretation, with consequent highly original results appropriate to the occasion.

EUROPA

Date of issue: 15 May 1984
The CEPT stamps were drawn by Fritz Wegner from a design by Jacky Larrivière.
The European Election stamps were designed by Fritz Wegner. Printed in photogravure by Harrison & Sons (High Wycombe) Limited.

Format:	horizontal
Size:	41mm x 30mm
Perforations:	15 x 14
Number per sheet:	100
Paper:	unwatermarked phosphor coated
Gum:	PVA Dextrin

ECONOMIC SUMMIT

International economic interdependence is a reality which virtually every national government in the world today has to accept. The time has long gone when one country could pursue its own economic policies without regard to the effect these might have on the national economies of others. This is particularly true of the developed nations of the Western world.

In the wake of the oil crisis in the early 1970s, many Western economies ran into major problems of high inflation and recession. As individual nations attempted to steer their way out of trouble, there was a growing feeling that only concerted international action would provide lasting solutions.

On the initiative of President Giscard d'Estaing of France, an economic summit was held at Rambouillet in 1975 to discuss this question. It was attended by the heads of state or government of the USA, France, UK, the Federal Republic of Germany, Japan and Italy.

This summit proved such a success that it has now become an annual event, with each participating government taking it in turn to play host. Membership was increased to include Canada in 1976 and the President of the European Economic Community in 1977, the first time the summit was held in London.

The Economic Summit which was hosted by the British Government at Lancaster House in June 1984 proved once again the value of these annual meetings. Like the summits held in Williamsburg, Versailles and Ottawa in the previous three years, it provided a relaxed atmosphere rarely found at international conferences. Such informality enabled the heads of government to discuss problems frankly and to coordinate policies on a wide range of economic issues. These included growth, inflation, unemployment, monetary matters, energy and international trade.

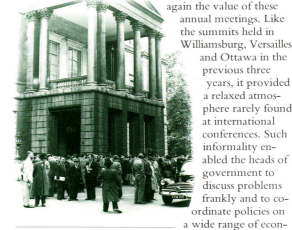

DELEGATES ARRIVE AT LANCASTER HOUSE FOR THE NINE-POWER CONFERENCE IN 1954 WHEN THE LANCASTER HOUSE TREATY WAS SIGNED

BENJAMIN DEAN WYATT, DESIGNER OF YORK HOUSE, NOW LANCASTER HOUSE

The choice of Lancaster House for the 1984 summit was very appropriate for this magnificent building has been the scene of many historical meetings and conferences since the end of the Second World War. In 1954, it was the setting for the Nine-Power Conference when the Lancaster House Treaty was signed in the State Drawing Room. It has also been the scene where final agreements were reached on the independence of a number of former British colonies such as Nigeria in 1958, Cyprus in 1959 and Zimbabwe in 1979.

Situated next to St James's Palace and overlooking the Mall in central London, Lancaster House is one of the finest examples of the early Victorian revival of French eighteenth-century architecture and styles. Designed originally as York House by Benjamin Dean Wyatt for the Duke of York, of 'grand old duke' fame, construction began in 1825. The Duke, however, was not to see its completion for he died two years later. One of the Duke's creditors, the Marquess of Stafford (later the Duke of Sutherland), purchased the unfinished building and had it completed by Sir Robert Smirke in the 1840s when it was renamed Stafford House. Sir Charles Barry, architect of the Houses of Parliament, was responsible for much of the lavish decoration used throughout the building.

In the latter half of the nineteenth century, Stafford House was one of the most fashionable centres for the aristocracy and leading political figures of the age. Impressed by the decor and furnishings, Queen Victoria remarked to the Duchess of Sutherland about 'coming from my house to your palace'. Among the many visitors at that time was the Italian patriot, Giuseppe Garibaldi, after whom one of the rooms was subsequently named.

PAUL HOGARTH – HIS FIRST ROYAL MAIL STAMP

The centrepiece of the building is the impressive staircase hall which rises to the full height of the building. Red and yellow imitation marble walls and fluted Corinthian columns supported by balconies rise up to meet the high, richly-decorated ceiling and coving. Other features of the building include the 120-foot long Great Gallery; the Veronese Room with its small ceiling

AN ENGRAVING PUBLISHED IN THE 'ILLUSTRATED LONDON NEWS' DEPICTING A MEETING HELD AT LANCASTER HOUSE TO DISCUSS ARRANGEMENTS FOR THE GREAT EXHIBITION OF 1851

ROYAL MAIL SPECIAL STAMPS · 1984

painting by that master; the Music Room where Chopin played before Queen Victoria in 1848; and the magnificent State Drawing Room with its beautiful coffered ceiling and elaborate fireplaces.

In 1912, the building was bought by Sir William Lever, later Lord Leverhulme, who renamed it Lancaster House in honour of his native county. He then bequeathed it to the nation and it became the home of the London Museum until 1941. After restoration following bomb damage in the 'Blitz', it was re-opened and now serves as a government hospitality centre for international conferences.

The London Economic Summit 1984 stamp was designed by Paul Hogarth who has done a great deal of architectural and landscape illustration. Although this is his first Royal Mail stamp, he has a well-established international reputation.

In the last twenty-five years, his work has taken him to many countries of the world, including China and

FOREIGN HEADS OF STATE AND GOVERNMENT AND THE EEC PRESIDENT PICTURED AT LANCASTER HOUSE WITH THE BRITISH PRIME MINISTER DURING THE 1984 SUMMIT

Russia. During that time he has had numerous books on his work published, the most notable perhaps being five books, *Drawing Architecture*, devoted to the American urban landscape, a subject which he finds endlessly fascinating. The most recent of these is *America Observed* on which he collaborated with Stephen Spender.

His other published works include *Brendan Behan's Island* on which he collaborated with the Irish playwright; *Majorca Observed* with Robert Graves; and *London a la Mode* with Malcolm Muggeridge. Paul is also well known for his book jacket designs, in particular all the Penguin editions of Graham Greene's novels in the last twenty years as well as the new edition of the Penguin Shakespeare.

For this stamp, Paul chose to illustrate the front entrance of Lancaster House with a full display of the national flags of the governments participating in the Summit.

Working from sketches and photographs which he took himself, he had to imagine what the scene would look like in June 1984 – dull, dreary February weather is hardly the best guide for the artist! As a result, he decided to use slightly exaggerated shadows across the front of the building as these helped to enhance the classical lines and character of the Lancaster House facade.

Because of the size of the building relative to the flags, there was a danger that the flags would not be sufficiently prominent when his illustration was reduced to stamp size. Consequently, he chose to make the flags somewhat larger than real size. The end result of Paul's work is a very pleasing illustration of what is one of London's most attractive buildings.

PAUL HOGARTH'S PRELIMINARY VISUAL OF LANCASTER HOUSE
THE FINAL ARTWORK FEATURED THE CENTRAL SECTION WHICH APPEARS ON THE STAMP

ECONOMIC SUMMIT

Date of issue: 5 June 1984

The stamp was designed by Paul Hogarth RDI and printed in photogravure by Harrison & Sons (High Wycombe) Limited.

Format: vertical
Size: 30mm x 41mm
Perforations: 14 x 15
Number per sheet: 100
Paper: unwatermarked phosphor coated
Gum: PVA Dextrin

ROYAL MAIL SPECIAL STAMPS · 1984

GREENWICH MERIDIAN

The decision 100 years ago to choose Greenwich as the world's prime meridian for longitude and time was probably the most significant centenary celebrated in 1984. This decision has had far-reaching consequences in the subsequent development of navigation techniques for shipping, aviation and space travel. Today, the Greenwich meridian is longitude zero for every country and is the basis of Co-ordinated Universal Time (UTC) used for time signals the world over.

This attractive and unusual set of lithographic stamps commemorates the centenary of the Greenwich meridian being accepted as the world standard. Designed by Sedley Place Design Limited and printed by The House of Questa, the stamps highlight the meridian's historical and present-day significance.

Before 1884, the search for the longitude had occupied the efforts of leading mathematicians, astronomers and navigators through the ages. Less than 200 years ago the term 'discovering the longitude' had a similar meaning to 'squaring the circle' – in other words, it implied a search for the impossible.

As long ago as 120 BC it was realised that finding differences of longitude would be possible only if the same event could be observed in two different places and the local times of the event compared. Such was the theory. In practice, the problems were to determine which event to observe and how to compare local times accurately.

Many theories were put forward as to which event was most suitable; eclipses of the moon and of Jupiter's satellites as well as measurements of the distances from the moon to the sun and certain zodiacal stars were just some of the ideas. All, however, proved to have major flaws.

The sea voyages of great navigators like Vasco da Gama and Columbus highlighted the need for a solution to the problem of finding longitude at sea. As ocean voyages increased in frequency, this need became more urgent. Latitude could be measured by observations of the Pole Star or of the Sun. With the discovery of the Cape Route to the Indies, however, it became essential to be able to navigate east-west distances just as well as north-south routes.

The Royal Observatory was built at Greenwich in 1675 and the first Astronomer Royal, Flamsteed, was charged with the task of providing the astronomical information needed for determining longitude at sea. Flamsteed realised that success would depend on years of observations with specialised telescopes because only then would information be available to the degree of accuracy required. An error of only one degree in longitude can mean a difference of about seventy miles in location. This is the difference between foundering on the Lizard and sailing safely into the mouth of the English Channel; many mariners paid for such an error with their lives.

Flamsteed's observations suggested that the Earth rotated on its axis at constant speed. Today, however, we know that this is not true – that is why our time is now determined by very accurate atomic clocks rather than the solar day. Tidal friction, the movement of the Earth's crust and mantle, melting and freezing of polar ice caps, and the wobble of the Earth on its axis are all contributing to make the Earth less than the perfect timekeeper. As a result, the year is decreasing by half a second per century; ultimately, there will be no need for a leap year, but not for a few million years yet!

Flamsteed concentrated upon observations of the stars while his successor, Halley, concentrated upon the moon. It was the fifth Astonomer Royal, Nevil Maskelyne, who finally collated the observations into a form suitable for navigators and first published them in the Nautical Almanac in 1766.

The Almanac, which is still published today, was based on Greenwich as representing zero longitude. Up to that time, longitude was usually expressed as degrees east or west of a departure point or destination. Now, for the first time, a common standard was established and within a century almost three quarters of the world's shipping used charts based on the Greenwich meridian.

The invention of the chronometer proved invaluable to the application of the Almanac since it enabled mariners to measure time at sea. The outstanding problems remained of how to know the right time in the first place and how to check the chronometers periodically thereafter. Here again, Greenwich was to play an important role in the solutions.

In 1833, a time-ball was erected at the Greenwich Observatory.

CROSS SECTION OF MAP SHOWING THE ZERO MERIDIAN LINE PASSING THROUGH GREENWICH

ARCHITECT AND ASTRONOMER, SIR CHRISTOPHER WREN, DESIGNED THE ROYAL OBSERVATORY IN 1675

A SIXTEENTH-CENTURY CROSS-STAFF USED FOR OBSERVING LUNAR DISTANCES AND MEASURING THE HEIGHTS OF BUILDINGS

FAST ROYAL MAIL COACHES CHANGED PEOPLE'S ATTITUDES TOWARD TIMEKEEPING. CLOCKS LIKE THIS ONE WERE CARRIED BY THE COACH GUARDS

At precisely one o'clock each day, the ball was dropped, thereby giving Greenwich time to ships in London's river and docks. It also made Greenwich time regularly available for the first time to those ashore who could see it.

Up to then, each part of the country had its own local time based on its own meridian – the time in London, for example, differing by some sixteen minutes from that in Plymouth. This caused no great inconvenience because travellers were few and the rate of travel was slow. The advent of fast Royal Mail coaches and, later, the introduction of even faster railways changed people's attitudes towards time and timekeeping.

By 1840, the multiplicity of local times was already causing problems for the Post Office, railways and newly-formed telegraph companies. That year, the Great Western Railway ordered that Greenwich time was to be observed at all its stations and in its time-tables, a decision which was repeated by other railway companies in the ensuing years.

In 1850, the Astonomer Royal, Airy, installed his famous transit telescope at Greenwich which was to find the time by observation of the so-called 'clock' stars. Two years later, he initiated a time distribution system based on electric clocks and telegraph links, whereby national standard time came into being. Though radio eventually replaced the telegraph, this system based on the idea that the rotating Earth is the fundamental timekeeper remained virtually unchanged until the advent of the atomic clock in the 1960s.

SIR GEORGE BIDDELL AIRY (ABOVE). THE LONGITUDE OF THE CABLE-LAYING SHIP 'GREAT EASTERN' (RIGHT) WAS MEASURED BY TIME SIGNALS FROM GREENWICH DURING ITS HISTORIC ATLANTIC VOYAGE IN 1866

The introduction of Greenwich Mean Time (GMT) was generally well received and by 1855 virtually all public clocks in Britain were set by GMT. There was, however, nothing in the statute book to define what was the time for legal purposes. Ten minutes before or after midnight could have important ramifications in insurance claims, inheritances and elections.

It was not until 1880 that GMT became legal time in Britain.

If the need for co-ordination of time-keeping was evident in Britain with a maximum longitude difference of about thirty minutes, it was even greater in the United States and Canada where there was more than three and a half hours' difference between the east and west coasts. This problem was highlighted in the 1870s by the fact that some eighty different time standards were in operation on US railroads.

In 1883, the United States and Canada decided to adopt a zonal time standard based upon the Greenwich meridian.

Meanwhile, geographers and scientists from many countries had been attempting to fix a common zero for longitude and time throughout the world. The multiplicity of national meridians based on capital cities or principal observatories was seen as a major hindrance, not only to science, but also to the development of international trade and communications.

Various international conferences were held to discuss this question, the most important of these being the International Meridian Conference called by the President of the USA and held in Washington in the autumn of 1884.

Greenwich had been the obvious favourite to become the common zero – the prime meridian – although claims continued to be made for alternative locations like Paris, Jerusalem and the Great Pyramids. However, the facts that Greenwich was already the established basis of longitude for almost all marine navigation throughout the world and had recently been adopted as the origin of standard time zones in the USA and Canada proved decisive. Following the Washington Conference, country after country decided to adopt a time-zone system based upon the world's new prime meridian, Greenwich.

Research for these stamps was carried out by Howard Waller and Terence Griffin of Sedley Place. The obvious starting place for this was the National Maritime Museum at Greenwich of which the Old Royal Observatory buildings now form a part. Carole Stott, Curator of the museum, was particularly helpful in this work. Another rich source of information proved to be the very interesting book 'Greenwich Time and the Discovery of the Longitude' by Derek Howse, former Head of Navigation and Astronomy at the National Maritime Museum.

Following this research, Howard Waller set himself the task of encapsulating both the historical and present-day significance of the Greenwich meridian.

SEDLEY PLACE DESIGN'S HOWARD WALLER – THE CONCEPT OF THE MERIDIAN'S MACRO AND MICRO PERSPECTIVE

From this he developed the concept of a zoom sequence showing the macro and micro perspective of the meridian, from its widest extra-terrestrial aspect right down to the exact spot which marks the location of the meridian itself.

Precision navigation and timekeeping are critical to the success of space travel. Consequently, it was appropriate that the first stamp should illustrate the vital contribution the Greenwich meridian has already made to man's wider exploration not only of Earth but of other planets as well. The illustration chosen for this stamp was a photograph of Earth taken from Apollo XI, the first manned lunar space flight.

Navigation at sea for the last two centuries or more owes much to the work of the Greenwich Observatory and its astronomers in establishing a common standard of longitude for mariners throughout the world and the publication of the Nautical Almanac. This close relationship between Greenwich and the sea is highlighted in the 20½p stamp by a navigational chart, now held by the National Maritime Museum, which was published around the time the International Meridian Conference made its momentous decision in 1884.

The third stamp shows the Old Royal Observatory and its historical relationship with the River Thames, a relationship reinforced by the time-ball system designed for the benefit of local shipping. This stamp proved particularly challenging as the aim was to photograph the Observatory with the river in the background but without showing any sky as the meridian line had to stay on earth. Special Civil Aviation Authority approval was necessary before photographer, Richard Cooke, was able to execute the photography from a low-flying twin-engined helicopter.

The final stamp shows the exact location of the prime meridian, the transit line of Airy's famous telescope. This telescope is mounted on an east-west axis so that it swings along a north-south line known as the meridian. Airy erected this nineteen feet east of the previous transit telescope, thereby moving the whole system of longitudes in Britain and, ultimately the world, east with it. The final drawing was produced by David Bristow of Sedley Place from Airy's original plans.

THE CREW OF APOLLO XI

The Greenwich Meridian stamps involved some very fine printing tolerances indeed. In particular, the red longitude lines running across each stamp appear to go right to the edge of the perforation. On closer examination, these actually stop fractionally short of the edge. Such delicacy is a tribute to the quality of The House of Questa's litho-printing capability.

GREENWICH MERIDIAN

Date of issue:	26 June 1984
	The four stamps were designed by Sedley Place Design and printed in offset lithography by The House of Questa
Format:	vertical
Size:	30mm × 41mm
Perforations:	14 × 15
Number per sheet:	100
Paper:	unwatermarked phosphor coated
Gum:	PVA Dextrin

CONTEMPORARY VIEWS OF THE OLD ROYAL OBSERVATORY PUBLISHED IN THE 'ILLUSTRATED LONDON NEWS'. THESE INCLUDE AIRY'S TRANSIT CIRCLE (TOP LEFT) WHICH HAS DEFINED THE GREENWICH MERIDIAN SINCE 1851, THE TIME BALL ON TOP OF THE EASTERN TURRET (CENTRE TOP) AND THE MEAN SOLAR STANDARD CLOCK (BOTTOM RIGHT) WHICH CONTROLLED THE DROPPING OF THE BALL

ROYAL MAIL

ROYAL MAIL SPECIAL STAMPS · 1984

The introduction of the Mail Coach Service in 1784 was a major milestone in British postal history. It is, therefore, very fitting that the stamps issued to commemorate the bicentenary of this event should themselves be a landmark in British philatelic development. A highly original style and distinctive quality have been achieved in this special se-tenant set of stamps which are a tribute to the individual skills and teamwork of everyone involved in its research, design and production.

The Mail Coach Service began on 2 August 1784 with a trial run from Bristol and Bath to London. This was to test a claim by John Palmer, then manager of theatres in Bristol and Bath, that his plan to use fast, armed coaches to carry the Royal Mail would transform the speed and security of mail services along the main highways out of London.

This experiment was to prove Palmer absolutely right and, within a few years, mail coaches were plying all the principal mail routes not only out of London but also between other major cities and towns. For the next sixty years, the 'Royal Mail' was a familiar sight in all parts of the country until it had to bow out to the increasing competition from the growing railway network.

Keith Bassford was commissioned to handle the design of these stamps with Stanley Paine undertaking the illustrations upon which the final engraved result would be based. Keith was responsible for the first day cover and presentation pack designs for the British Theatre set in 1982 and last year's British Army issue while Stanley designed and illustrated the British Cars stamps of 1982.

The logical starting point for their research was the archives at Postal Headquarters in St Martin's-le-Grand where they found archivist, Jean Farrugia, an enthusiastic participant in unearthing historical material about the coaching era. It was this research that led them to the coaching prints of James Pollard which were to form the inspiration for the design of the stamps.

Born in 1792, the son of an established engraver, Pollard grew up in Islington close to the two great mail routes through North London, a proximity which probably accounted for his life-long passion for painting the great mail coaches of the day. He, in fact, spent a great deal of time travelling around the country by coach in pursuit of his art. He was certainly no stranger to the hazards of this mode of travel as he was thrown off a coach on its way to Goodwood races on one occasion when the horses bolted.

All the stamps, except for the one depicting the Bath Mail, were inspired by Pollard's pictures. It is improbable that he actually witnessed the coaching incidents portrayed, in particular the attack by a lioness on the Exeter Mail. However, this scene was drawn from the account of an eye-witness, Joseph Pike, guard of the Exeter Mail on that night in 1816 when the lioness had escaped from a travelling menagerie. All the passengers made the safety of the inn except

THIS GUIDE SHOWED THE ROUTES AND MAIN POINTS OF INTEREST TO BE SEEN WHEN TRAVELLING BY ROYAL MAIL COACH

JOHN PALMER – HIS THEORY WAS TO TRANSFORM THE SPEED AND SECURITY OF THE ROYAL MAIL SERVICES THROUGHOUT THE COUNTRY

EACH LEATHER LETTER BAG HAD A BRASS DESTINATION IDENTIFIER (LEFT). ONLY RARELY DID THE MAIL NOT ARRIVE (ABOVE)

COACH RECEIPTS OF THE MAIL COACH ERA. THE COACHES WERE OPERATED BY CONTRACTORS WITH THE GUARD BEING THE ONLY POST OFFICE EMPLOYEE ON BOARD

MAIL COACHES RAN UNTIL 1846. THE LAST MAIL COACH GUARD, JAMES NOBBS, IS PICTURED ABOVE

THE MAIL COACH USED FOR THE BICENTENNIAL BRISTOL TO LONDON RE-RUN IN AUGUST 1984 WAS A REPLICA OF 'QUICKSILVER' (ABOVE), WHICH WAS THE FASTEST MAIL COACH EVER, AND THE ONLY ONE TO HAVE A NAME

A WOODCUT BY SIR WILLIAM NICHOLSON FROM 'ALMANAC OF TWELVE SPORTS' SHOWING A MAIL COACH OF THE ERA

for one. In the panic he was locked out and never did regain his sanity!

It had been decided from the outset that these stamps would be printed using Harrison's combined recess (intaglio) and photogravure process, only the third time a Royal Mail stamp would be printed by this method. The recess process is particularly suitable where very fine detail is required in reproduction. It does, however, demand close liaison between designer, illustrator and engraver, and engraver and printer to ensure the very best results.

The format of the stamps was established by Keith Bassford's design. It was then Stanley Paine's task to interpret the Pollard prints to suit this format. Every print had to be redrawn and scaled down so that each coach would appear approximately the same size. Other elements such as horses, backgrounds and landscapes were then brought into the right perspective. Additional details either missing or obscured in the original prints had to be included.

When the design and illustrations were completed, it was the engraver's turn to make his contribution. For this stamp, the Post Office chose Czeslaw Slania, probably the leading stamp engraver in the world today.

The engraver's first task is to take the artwork which is six times stamp size and trace the outline of this onto a zinc plate. This plate is put into a pantograph which reduces the outline image to stamp size. The engraver then transfers the image to a soft steel plate on which he will make the engraving.

Using a burin and a magnifying glass the engraver next interprets every single element in the illustrator's artwork by cutting into the steel. In the darkest areas, he needs to cut up to seven lines a millimetre! As if that were not difficult enough, he has, of course, to engrave the picture in reverse.

The engraver also has to take account of a number of other factors. In particular, he must know exactly the method and

JAMES POLLARD (ABOVE LEFT) AND HIS PRINT OF THE LIONESS ATTACKING THE EXETER MAIL IN 1816. THE ANIMAL'S REPUTATION APPEARS TO HAVE BEEN ENHANCED BY THIS FEAT, IF ONE IS TO JUDGE BY THE POSTER (ABOVE RIGHT)

KEITH BASSFORD'S INITIAL CONCEPTS (TOP) WERE DEVELOPED TO PROVIDE A FRAMEWORK FOR STANLEY PAINE'S ROUGH ILLUSTRATION (ABOVE). THE TRACING (LEFT) BY STANLEY PAINE IS TAKEN FROM THE COMPLETED DESIGN WHICH IS SIX TIMES STAMP SIZE

ROYAL MAIL SPECIAL STAMPS · 1984

THE OUTLINE OF THE ARTWORK (ABOVE) IS REDUCED TO STAMP SIZE AND TRANSFERRED, IN REVERSE, ONTO A SOFT STEEL PLATE (LEFT). THE ENGRAVER CUTS INTO THIS WITH A KNIFE OR BURIN — IN THE DARKEST AREAS HE NEEDS TO CUT UP TO SEVEN LINES A MILLIMETRE

DESIGNER AND ILLUSTRATOR
KEITH BASSFORD (LEFT)
AND STANLEY PAINE (ABOVE)

direction of ink wiping that is to be used on the recess printing process for that stamp. This will enable him to avoid cutting lines in the same plane as the wipe and having the ink swept out during printing. To prevent this happening, he will normally cut at an angle to the wiping plane. The skill involved in the engraving process can be measured simply by looking at a stamp under a magnifying glass.

One might wonder how it is possible to render such fine lines in pen and ink at stamp size, let alone engraving them in steel and in reverse for final printing.

ROYAL MAIL

Date of issue: 31 July 1984
The five se-tenant stamps were designed by Keith Bassford and Stanley Paine and engraved by Czeslaw Slania. They were printed in recess and photogravure by Harrison & Sons (High Wycombe) Limited.

Format:	horizontal
Size:	41mm x 30mm
Perforations:	15 x 14
Number per sheet:	100
Paper:	unwatermarked phosphor coated
Gum:	PVA Dextrin

BRITISH COUNCIL

Stamp themes generally fall into two broad categories. There are those with fairly narrow or obvious aspects which challenge the designer to find new ways to interpret them and to sustain visual interest across a set of stamps. Conversely, there are stamp

subjects, like the British Council, with such a broad range of applications that the designer faces an entirely different problem – namely, how to capture the essence of the subject.

The British Council undertakes a multiplicity of cultural, educational and technical tasks in its aim to promote an enduring understanding and appreciation of Britain throughout the world. And these stamps demonstrate just how well the designers, Newell and Sorrell, have managed to distil such wide-ranging activities in a way that is truly representative of the Council's function and significance today.

These are the first Royal Mail stamps designed by Newell and Sorrell, a young design group based in London. The company's philosophy of approaching projects in an analytical way was evident from the start of their work on these stamps. They undertook extensive research into the British Council's function and present-day activities.

Founded in 1934, the British Council has grown in its first fifty years to become an important cultural dimension to Britain's overseas representation, thereby creating beneficial and lasting links, not only with our closest international partners, but also with nations whose systems are very different from our own. Through its international

HOW A STAMP IS BORN – NEWELL & SORRELL'S INITIAL CONCEPTS (TOP LEFT) LEAD ON TO PENCIL SKETCH (LEFT) AND COLOUR ILLUSTRATION (ABOVE) BY BRIAN SANDERS

organisation, the Council is able to demonstrate the unique character of British people and achievements, not in a narrow jingoistic way but in a spirit of mutual co-operation and interchange of ideas with other people.

At home, the British Council is governed by people representing the widest aspects of British education, arts, science, agriculture, medicine and industry. Through a network of regional offices, committees for Scotland and Wales and specialist advisory committees, the Council keeps in close touch with achievements and resources in all of these areas. From its London headquarters, the Director General controls over 4,000 staff and specialists in Britain and in eighty countries overseas.

The Council is an independent body operating under Royal Charter with The Queen as its patron. Funding comes mainly from British Government grants and it is extensively employed by the Overseas Development Administration and major international agencies like the United Nations to administer aid programmes in human skills and training. Its consultancy services and training programmes are in increasing

demand from overseas institutions and organisations.

Following extensive research, Newell & Sorrell decided to concentrate on the educative aspect of the Council's work. The examples illustrated on the stamps were chosen because, individually, they showed where the Council devotes the greater part of its effort and, collectively, they clearly represent the spirit of the Council's commitment. Each stamp incorporates an illustration of this work set against a background showing its wider aspects.

The illustrations are by Brian Sanders whose work is very familiar to collectors of Royal Mail stamps since he designed the British Police issue in 1978, the Fishing Industry set in 1980 and Youth Movements in 1981.

The 17p stamp shows a Nigerian doctor who has received postgraduate medical training in Britain under British Council agreements with the Overseas Development Administration and the Government of Nigeria. The background pattern consists of the formulae of drugs manufactured in Britain which are pertinent to Africa – this information was taken from a number of medical books, redrawn and put together.

Some 30,000 people from over 180 countries come to Britain every year on

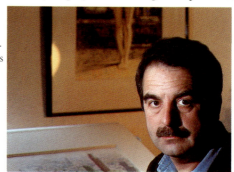

BRIAN SANDERS – PORTRAYING PEOPLE WITH A SENSE OF REALISM

ROYAL MAIL SPECIAL STAMPS · 1984

training courses and study visits with British Council help. At the same time, the Council sends more than 15,000 specialists abroad to 103 countries to teach, advise and consult.

The Council's valuable work in promoting British arts abroad is depicted on the 22p stamp. A British violinist is shown playing at the Herod Atticus Theatre in Athens with the Parthenon in the background. The surrounding pattern is taken from the score of Sir Michael Tippett's opera *Midsummer Marriage*. Sir Michael, one of Britain's most eminent living composers, who celebrated his eightieth birthday in 1984, has often collaborated with the British Council. The Council has sponsored recordings of many of his works, including the one shown on this stamp.

Over 300 tours are organised annually by Council staff to ensure that the best of British traditional and contemporary art, drama, music, film, poetry, opera and dance is presented overseas. Fine art, documentary and general exhibitions are also sponsored abroad and some 20,000 films on a wide range of subjects with a British interest are shown in the Council's libraries.

The importance of the Council's work in technical and vocational training, as part of the national programmes of developing countries, is illustrated on the 31p stamp. This shows British and Sri Lankan colleagues engaged in the Government of Sri Lanka Construction Industry Training Board project for which the Council is providing consultancy and training services. The background is taken from a British Building

AN EXHIBITION OF BRITISH WORKS OF ART IN PARIS ORGANISED BY THE BRITISH COUNCIL

Construction training manual.

Helped by staff from the former Technical Education and Training Organisation for Overseas Countries, the Council administers the training of thousands of people from other countries for the Overseas Development Administration's Technical Co-oper-

NEWELL & SORRELL – RESEARCH AN ESSENTIAL ELEMENT OF THEIR DESIGN PHILOSOPHY

ation Training Programme, foreign governments and international agencies.

English is the key language to advancement and business success in many parts of the world and its teaching is one of the Council's prime activities. Each year nearly a quarter of a million students learn the language with Council help either in Britain or at one of the Council's thirty-nine centres in twenty-nine countries. The Council also operates one of the finest lending, reference and information services in the world through its network of 111 libraries which hold a total of two million books, periodicals and other materials as well as computer-linked information retrieval systems.

These two vital aspects of the

TV PRODUCERS FROM OVERSEAS ON A BBC/OPEN UNIVERSITY TV PRODUCTION COURSE SPONSORED BY THE BRITISH COUNCIL (LEFT). A BRITISH COUNCIL BOOK PRESENTATION AT A SCHOOL IN ZIMBABWE (BELOW)

Council's work are demonstrated in the 34p stamp. The illustration depicts the services being used in one of the Council's libraries in the Middle East while the background, appropriately, shows the definition of the word 'English' taken from the shorter *Oxford English Dictionary*.

BRITISH COUNCIL

Date of issue: 25 September 1984

The four stamps were designed by Newell and Sorrell Design Ltd and printed in photogravure by Harrison & Sons (High Wycombe) Limited.

Format:	horizontal
Size:	41mm × 30mm
Perforations:	15 × 14
Number per sheet:	100
Paper:	unwatermarked phosphor coated
Gum:	PVA Dextrin

CHRISTMAS

Although the nativity of Christ is one of the most familiar stories in the Western world, what we often do not realise is the extent to which our image of this event has been influenced by artists through the ages. The work of the Old Masters from Europe and the Pre-Raphaelites, in particular, has had a marked effect on how the very first Christmas nearly 2,000 years ago is perceived today.

A great deal of the art devoted to the events surrounding Christ's birth says as much about the artistic styles and attitudes of the times in which the paintings were executed, as it does about what actually happened. Even in the last thirty years, we have seen contrasting interpretations of the Bible in films and television series where the differences in emphasis and detail have much to do with the cinematic styles and techniques in vogue at the time of production.

What is unusual about 1984's Christmas stamps is the fact that artist, Yvonne Gilbert, instead of following the traditional or classical interpretation of the Nativity scenes, has taken herself back in time to portray the events as clearly as if they had happened yesterday.

It was entirely appropriate that 1984's Christmas stamps should retell the origins of Christianity since it was Christian Heritage Year. Many remarkable men and women have been inspired by their Christian beliefs to change and enrich our society and Christian Heritage celebrates the contributions they have made to the betterment of their fellow men and women.

When Yvonne Gilbert was asked to design the Christmas stamps, her brief was to imagine herself a photographer sent back in time to record the events of the Nativity for posterity. It certainly was not an easy task, not least because it meant she had to distance herself from the popular image of the Nativity which has evolved over the centuries.

Yvonne is an established artist with a particular interest in fashion and period costume – an interest which was to prove extremely useful in determining what the people of Palestine wore at the time of Christ's birth – and these are the first Royal Mail stamps she has designed.

Her starting point, of course, was the Bible which she read as if it were the first time, blotting out as many preconceived ideas as possible. Only two of the four Gospels, those of Luke and Matthew, actually give an account of the Nativity and there are considerable differences in detail between each account. Matthew, for example, relates the story of the Magi, or astrologers, but Luke has nothing to say about anyone bearing gifts. Luke describes the shepherds and the manger while Matthew makes no mention of either.

The familiar story of the Nativity is a blend of the Gospels according to Luke and Matthew. Consequently, the Adoration of the Shepherds and the Adoration of the Magi were often combined in early Christian art.

In Venetian paintings, the shepherds were portrayed with their women and dogs as well as their sheep. While Raphael showed his shepherds living in a kind of 'Greek' arcadia, later Italian painters portrayed them wearing sheepskin jackets, typical not of Palestine but of their own part of Italy.

Most paintings of the Magi represent them as three kings, an interpretation founded on early church legends, with the King of Ethiopia invariably portrayed as a negro or Moor. The gifts of gold, frankincense and myrrh were symbols of homage to Jesus as King, God and man.

Although the Gospels relate that Mary and Joseph hailed from Galilee, there is no physical description of either or of the baby Jesus. Portrayals of Jesus, Mary and Joseph in Nativity paintings through the ages show wide variations in interpretation, though they are often painted with haloes.

Yvonne Gilbert

YVONNE GILBERT'S EARLY STAMP-SIZE PENCIL ROUGHS

ARTIST YVONNE GILBERT – HER INTEREST IN COSTUME WAS TO PROVE INVALUABLE

ONE OF THE MOST FAMILIAR MODERN INTERPRETATIONS OF THE BIBLE STORY WAS FRANCO ZEFFIRELLI'S TELEVISION SERIES 'JESUS OF NAZARETH'

BOTTICELLI'S IDEALISED MADONNA AND CHILD IN 'MYSTIC NATIVITY'

PEN AND INK DEVELOPMENTS OF YVONNE GILBERT'S EARLY PENCIL ROUGHS SHOWING DIFFERENT NATIVITY SCENES

ROYAL MAIL SPECIAL STAMPS · 1984

INK ROUGH OF THE 22P STAMP DEPICTING THE SHEPHERD BOY AND LAMB (LEFT) AND THE COMPLETED ILLUSTRATION (BELOW) SENSITIVELY EXECUTED IN COLOURED PENCIL

undertook considerable research into the type of clothing which a couple of Mary and Joseph's social standing would have worn. From this, she was able to determine that it was almost certainly a fabric in a subdued colour achieved through the use of vegetable dyes. She was also able to establish what the rough clothing of a Judean shepherd boy looked like.

Choosing five instantly recognisable scenes from the Nativity story, Yvonne designed these as realistically as possible. Her major achievement with these very attractive Christmas stamps has been to instil a remarkably fresh, almost photographic quality to scenes which appear as if they happened only yesterday.

REFERENCE PHOTOGRAPHS OF LAMB (LEFT) AND DONKEY (ABOVE) WHICH YVONNE GILBERT USED FOR HER FINAL ILLUSTRATIONS

CHRISTMAS

Date of issue: 20 November 1984

The five stamps were designed by Yvonne Gilbert and printed in photogravure by Harrison & Sons (High Wycombe) Limited.

Format:	horizontal
Size:	41mm x 30mm
Perforations:	15 x 14
Number per sheet:	100
Paper:	unwatermarked phosphor coated
Gum:	PVA Dextrin

ACKNOWLEDGEMENTS

HERALDRY
Page 4. Fenwick Roll (Ian Yeomans/Susan Griggs Agency); Richard III (National Portrait Gallery)
Page 5. Coronation (Popperfoto); College of Arms and its coat of arms (The College of Arms)

CATTLE
Page 6. Rosette (The Hereford Herd Book Society)
Page 7. 'Farmer with his Prize Heifer' artist unknown, c.1830 (Crane Kalman Gallery)

URBAN RENEWAL
Page 9. Engraving of old Durham/Milburngate Shopping Centre (Building Design Partnership)

EUROPA
Page 10. Parliament in session (The European Parliament); Fritz Wegner and Jacky Larrivière (Post Office Archives)
Page 11. 'ESPRIT' programme (The European Parliament)

ECONOMIC SUMMIT
Page 12. Benjamin Wyatt (RIBA picture library); 1954 Nine-Power Conference (Popperfoto);
Grand staircase at Lancaster House (London Illustrated News);
Page 13. Heads of State at 1984 Economic Summit (Popperfoto)

GREENWICH MERIDIAN
Page 14. Sir Christopher Wren (RIBA picture library); 16th century illustration from 'Greenwich Time' by Derek Howse (Oxford University Press);
Map section (John Bartholomew & Son Ltd); Mail coach clock (Post Office Archives)
Page 15. Sir George Biddell Airy/The Great Eastern (London Illustrated News)
Page 16. Views of Old Royal Observatory (London Illustrated News); Crew of Apollo XI (Space Frontiers)

ROYAL MAIL
Page 17. John Palmer/James Nobbs/brass label/printed ephemera (Post Office Archives)
Coaching print by William Nicholson from 'Almanac of Twelve Sports' (Heinemann)

BRITISH COUNCIL
Page 20. Sculpture/book presentation/T.V. producers (The British Council)

CHRISTMAS
Page 22. 'Jesus of Nazareth' (ITC Entertainment Ltd)
Page 23. 'Mystic Nativity' Botticelli, 1500 (The National Gallery)

STAMP POSITIONING GUIDE

Heraldry · Page 5

Economic Summit
Page 13

Greenwich Meridian · Page 15

Cattle · Page 7

Royal Mail · Page 19

Urban Renewal · Page 9

British Council · Page 21

Europa · Page 11

Christmas · Page 23